BOUNCERS

1990's REMIX

BOUNCERS

REMIX

by John Godber

JOSEF WEINBERGER PLAYS

LONDON

Bᴏᴜɴᴄᴇʀs Rᴇᴍɪx
First published in 1987
by Josef Weinberger Ltd (pka Warner/Chappell Plays Ltd)
12-14 Mortimer Street, London, W1T 3JJ
www.josef-weinberger.com
general.info@jwmail.co.uk

This edition first published 1993
Reprinted 1997, 1999, 2001, 2002, 2003, 2006, 2008

ISBN 0 85676 172 9

Printed in England by Commercial Colour Press plc, Hainault, Essex.

BOUNCERS was first presented by Hull Truck Theatre Company at the Assembly Rooms, Edinburgh as part of the Edinburgh Festival Fringe on 11 August, 1984, transferring to the Donmar Warehouse Theatre, London in September. The production was nominated for 'Comedy of the Year' in the 1985 Olivier Awards, and the cast was as follows:

LUCKY ERIC	Peter Geeves
JUDD	Richard Ridings
RALPH	Richard May
LES	Andrew Dunn

Directed by John Godber

It was subsequently produced by Hull Truck Theatre Company and Armand Gerrard Management at the Arts Theatre, London, opening on 22 July 1986.

An earlier version of BOUNCERS was originally commissioned by the Yorkshire Actors Company and first performed at the Rotherham Arts Centre on 25 March, 1983, with the following cast:

LUCKY ERIC	Peter Geeves
JUDD	John Graham Davies
RALPH	Paul Rhys
LES	Andrew Dunn

Directed by Andrew Winters

This version of BOUNCERS first performed in 1991, directed by John Godber for Hull Truck, with the following cast:

LUCKY ERIC	Charlie Dickinson
JUDD	Adrian Hood
RALPH	Ian Rogerson
LES	Mick Callaghan

In the United States, BOUNCERS has won 7 Los Angeles Drama Critics Circle Awards and 5 Joseph Jefferson Awards in Chicago.

photograph by Steve Morgan from the Hull Truck Theatre Company production of Bouncers at the Donmar Warehouse, 1986

ACT ONE

Eric and the bouncers have been parading the auditorium. As the music plays they enter the stage. An open space. Les, Judd and Ralph stand upstage. Eric addresses the audience. There is a sense of menace throughout.

Eric   Ladies and gentlemen, we present the Bouncers remix.

Judd/
Ralph/   B O U N C E R S (*Elongating the 'S'.*)
Les

Eric   We welcome you to a vision
Of the nineties' urban night-life
To stag nights and hen-do's
To drunken crying girls and gallons of booze

Judd/
Ralph/   (*singing*) Celebration time, come on!
Les

Eric   It's always frustrating
For the oldest swingers in town
Yes all human life is inevitably here
In a midnight circus
And I must make it clear
That the beer is pricy, the music pulsating
The atmosphere is intoxicating
We four will try to illustrate
The sort of things that happen late
At night in every town
When the pubs are shut
And the beers' been downed . . .

NOW DOWN AT THE DISCO IS THE PLACE TO BE
THE LIGHTS ARE SO BRIGHT
LIKE A COLOUR TV
THE MUSIC IS LOUD
AND THE BEER FLOWS FREE
IT'S A DISCO PLACE FOR YOU AND ME

NOW ON THE DOOR, YOU PAY YOUR MONEY
THE PLACE IS PACKED, THE PLACE IS FUNNY
LOOK AT THE GIRLS . . .

ALL   MMMMMMMMM . . .

ERIC   SMELL THEIR HONEY
COME TO THE PLACE
WHERE THE BEAT PULSATES
IN THE HEAT OF THE NIGHT
THE WALLS GYRATE
IN THE BOWELS OF HELL
THE SCENT IS STRONG
THERE'S SEX IN THE AIR
AND THE HUNT IS ON
AND THE CHILDREN OF ENGLAND
SING THEIR SONG

ALL   (*slowly*) HERE WE GO, HERE WE GO, HERE WE
GO . . .

(*A pause.*)

LES/   WELL YOU FINISH WORK
JUDD

RALPH/   WELL IT'S FRIDAY NIGHT
ERIC

LES/   SO YOU'VE GOT YOUR PAY . . .
JUDD

RALPH/   AND YOU FEEL ALRIGHT
ERIC

ALL   PUMP UP THE BITTER
PUMP UP THE BITTER
PUMP UP THE BITTER
DOWN EIGHT PINTS
YOU DON'T CA CARE CARE
YOU DON'T CA CARE CARE
YOU DON'T CA CARE CARE
COZ IT'S FRIDAY NIGHT

ERIC   I SAID HIP HIPPY

JUDD   GIP GIPPY

ALL   HIP GIP HOP BOP
       DRINK THAT SLOP AND DON'T YOU STOP

ERIC   GET DOWN GET UP GET IN GET OUT

JUDD/
ERIC   GET DOWN GET UP GET IN GET OUT

LES/
JUDD/
ERIC   GET DOWN GET UP GET IN GET OUT

ALL   GET DOWN GET UP GET IN GET OUT

ERIC   THE BOUNCERS ARE MEAN
       IN THEIR BLACK AND WHITE
       THE FELLAS ARE PISSED
       BUT THEIR FISTS ARE TIGHT
       BUT THE CHICKS ARE LOOSE

ALL   (*as women*) 'COZ IT'S FRIDAY NIIIIGHT . . .

ERIC   WE GOT SOUL

ALL   RAP

ERIC   WE GOT SOUL

ALL   HOUSE RAP

ERIC   WE PLAY A LOT OF OTHER STUFF

JUDD   THAT SOUNDS LIKE CRAP

ALL   (*building*) GET DOWN GET UP
       GET IN GET OUT
       GET DOWN GET UP
       GET IN GET OUT
       GET DOWN GET UP
       GET IN GET OUT

ERIC   IF YOU COME DOWN HERE
       WEARING JEANS

JUDD   YOU CAN'T GET IN

ALL   KNOW WHAT HE MEANS?
            GOTTA HAVE A TIE, GOTTA HAVE A SUIT
            GOTTA LOOK CUTE OR YOU'LL GET THE
            BOOT
            GOTTA HAVE A TIE GOTTA HAVE A SUIT
            GOTTA LOOK CUTE OR YOU'LL GET THE
            BOOT

            (*They are stage centre. A spotlight picks them out.
            STEVE WRIGHT SHOW.*)

LES   You're listening to Radio One with Steve Wright.
            "Hello Steve it's Gervaise here, keep your tongue
            out and I'll call you right back."

ALL   Ten fifty three. Ten eighty nine. Radio One FM.

RALPH   (*as* BOWIE) Tell me what the time is, tell me what
            the temperature is.

LES   Yes that was the 'Bouncers', strange name for a
            group that.

RALPH   Yes yes yesh boy yesh boy get a pen . . . get a
            pen . . .

JUDD   Fillet o' fish, fillet o' fish, give me a fish to fillet.

LES   Yes. That record is going down very well in the
            discos so I shall certainly be playing it tonight at my
            gig in Littlehampton.

RALPH   Yes indeed.

ALL   Yes we do.

JUDD   Let's have that off.

            (*Suddenly the scene changes and the bouncers
            become female customers in a ladies' hairdresser.
            RALPH sits under a hairdryer, reading a magazine.*)

ERIC [MAUREEN] *is having his hair washed by* JUDD [CHERYL]. LES *is offstage*.)

JUDD That Steve Wright gets up my ring . . . and he's so popular because people keep ringing him up. Do you listen to it, Maureen?

ERIC No, Cheryl love. It gets on my bloody nerves. I like that Bruno Brooks and Gaz za za Davies.

JUDD This new *Alberto Balsam* should do wonders for your hair, Maureen.

ERIC Do you think so?

JUDD Oh yeah.

ERIC I want to look nice for tonight.

JUDD Going anywhere special?

ERIC It's Rosie's twenty-first. It should be a good do.

JUDD I hope it is, love.

ERIC You know her. She comes in here. She works at our place. Four of us are going down to *Mr Cinders*.

JUDD Oh, I've heard some good reports about that place.

ERIC Yes. It's alright.

ALL Yes. It's alright.

ERIC It's the best place round here.

JUDD It's all plush, isn't it?

ERIC Yeah. You've got to get there early to get in. It gets packed out. Like the black hole of bloody Calcutta.

(LES *enters the hairdresser's, out of breath. He has become* ROSIE.)

LES Hi ya.

ALL   Hi ya.

LES   Chuffin' hell. Talk about being rushed off your feet. Look at the time and I've only just finished.

ERIC   What've you been up to, Rosie?

LES   An order came in at ten to four.

ERIC   Chuffin' cheek.

LES   Friday and all. And my bleeding birthday.

ALL   Cheeky getts.

LES   Can you fit me in, Cheryl?

JUDD   I can't, I'm afraid, love. I'm chock-a-block till seven.

RALPH   I told her to book.

JUDD   I'm going out myself . . . *Dagonara Casino.*

ERIC   Gambling?

JUDD   Well . . .

ALL   Bloody 'ell.

LES   I'll just have to be late, that's all. I'll nip over to Barbara's. She might be able to fit me in. I'll see you down here later, Maureen.

ERIC   Alright, luv.

LES   Tara, luvs.

ALL   Tara.

LES   (*to audience*) Tara everyone.

ERIC   She's a dizzy sod, that Rosie.

RALPH   (*getting uncomfortable under the hairdryer*) How much longer, Cheryl?

JUDD   Bloody hell. She's on fire!

ERIC   Cheryl.

JUDD   Bloody hell. I wish you'd get your hair cut.

ERIC   I've got a new sort of skirt thing. It's nice, a bit tight, but so what? Ski pants as well.

JUDD   C & A?

ERIC   No.

JUDD   Top Shop?

ERIC   No chance. Got it from Chelsea Girl.

JUDD/
RALPH   Chelsea Girl.

JUDD   Oh yeah. They're lovely. I've got one in a sort of maroon.

ERIC/
RALPH   Maroon.

JUDD   I got them in the sale.

ERIC   How much were they?

ALL   Barbers!

(*Although the scene remains exactly the same we are now in a barber's.* JUDD *is a brusque barber.* ERIC *is in the chair.* RALPH *reads a dirty magazine.*)

JUDD   Come and get your hair cut if you dare.

RALPH   Jesus Christ! Where is he?

ERIC   I can't see him.

JUDD   I'm over here, lads. Right. Who wants what? You young lads want a proper haircut. Well, for three fifty you can have the Vinnie Jones look. Very popular with the thugs. Or for three fifty you can have the Elephant Man cut.

ERIC	What's the Elephant Man cut?
JUDD	It makes one side of your head look bigger than the other.
RALPH	Funny barber.
JUDD	You said it.
RALPH	I wouldn't let him near me.
ERIC	Why?
RALPH	Look at his own hair.
JUDD	(*ignoring them*) Or you can have the Tony Curtis haircut look.
ERIC	Hey, what's the Tony Curtis haircut look?
JUDD	All off. Totally bald. Egghead cut.
ERIC	Tony Curtis doesn't have his hair cut like that . . .
JUDD	He does if he comes in here. Funny, eh? Funny, lads, eh?
ERIC	Just cut it, will yer and cut the gags.
	(ERIC *gets in the chair and* JUDD *begins to cut his hair.*)
JUDD	Going somewhere, are we?
ERIC	Disco.
JUDD	How old are you?
RALPH	(*looking at a magazine*) Juddy hell! Look at the body on that.
ERIC	I'm nineteen.
JUDD	Got a woman?
RALPH	I hope that she's down there tonight.

ERIC   I might have at two o'clock.

JUDD   Make sure that you don't get an ugly one.

RALPH   There's only ugly ones left at two o'clock.

ERIC   Bollocks, Jerry.

JUDD   Watch the language, you.

RALPH   What are you doing to his hair? He can't go out like
            that . . . hey you can keep away from me, you
            bleeding maniac.

JUDD   Anything on?

ERIC   No thanks.

JUDD   Anything for the weekend?

RALPH   Yeah, I'll have a gross.

ERIC   What time are we starting?

RALPH   Time they do open.

            (LES *enters.*)

LES   I'm here, you dreamers.

ALL   Kev.

ERIC   Kev, ready for the big night.

LES   Ready as I'll ever be.

RALPH   Hey. I am dying for it. I've starved myself all week.

ERIC   He's a dirty sod.

LES   Seven o'clock in the Taverners, right?

ERIC/   Right.
RALPH

LES   Alright.

| ERIC/ | Alright. |
| RALPH | |

LES   Where's Terry?

JUDD   I'm here.

(JUDD *switches from playing the barber to playing*
TERRY. *The scene changes to a street corner where*
they all wait for TERRY.)

ALL   I thought he was the barber.

JUDD   Just finished a mindless day of wood stackin',
           talking about the races at Chepstow, the dogs at
           White City and the chances of England winning the
           World Cup . . .

ALL   (*chanting*) Engla-and.

JUDD   . . . ready for the night-time. Mindless girl watching
           and a chance perhaps of the old sniff of perfume and
           feel of inside thigh; milky-white thighs and
           bloodshot eyes. It's no surprise that I'm dying for it.

ALL   See you down there at seven.

ALL   Terry-Jerry-Kev-Baz-

JUDD   Be young -

ERIC   Be foolish -

LES   But be happy -

ALL   Be da da da da da da da da . . .

RALPH   And be careful not to catch it!

ALL   Bollocks!

(*The actors now become the lads getting ready for*
the big night out.)

ERIC   Baz, that is it. Friday night, fit for a fight. Get down
           there. Have a skinful. Might have a Chinese, or a
           chicken-in-the-basket. Maybe a hot-dog. Might risk

it. Got my dole money saved up. Try and pull some skirt. Give her a pup.

RALPH   I'm looking cool. I'm looking great. Wish I didn't have that spot. (*He squeezes an imaginary spot.*) Gotcha! Blackheads. Slap some *Clearasil* on my face. Not bad, Jerry. Not bad at all, mate.

ERIC   Hope I don't get stabbed again.

JUDD   Time is it?

LES   Jesus Christ . . .

RALPH   Ten to seven.

LES   Gonna be late.

RALPH   Time for another quick check.

(*They all stand in a row and check the various parts of their bodies.*)

ERIC   Hair?

ALL   Check.

JUDD   Tie?

ALL   Check.

ERIC   Aftershave? Jason Donovan uses this.

ALL   (*sing*) Sealed With a Kiss . . . Check.

ERIC   Talc on genitals?

ALL   Check.

ERIC   Clean underpants?

RALPH   Well . . .

LES   They'll do.

ERIC   Money?

ALL   Double check.

LES   Condoms?

ALL   Checkaroonie.

JUDD   Breath?

(*They all breathe out and try and smell their own breath.*)

ALL   Ugh! Beer should drown that.

JUDD   Right. That's it then. We're ready. Catch the bus at the end of our street.

RALPH   Ding ding.

LES   Fares please.

ERIC   Bollocks.

JUDD   Get downtown to start the pub crawl. When we get there it's packed already. I see me mates. Baz, Jerry an' Kev an' me into the Taverners.

(*During the following sequence the lads attempt to get served. Their actions should convey the bustling, pushy atmosphere of a pub.*)

JUDD   Four pints, please!

ALL   (*as they down the first pint of the evening*) ONE!

LES   'Course I'm eighteen.

ERIC   Get some crisps.

JUDD   Four bags of beef.

RALPH   Look at tits on that.

ALL   (*to audience*) Social comment.

JUDD   Four pints, pal.

ALL   TWO!

RALPH	Hey, who's pushing?
ERIC	Are you being served?
LES	Hey up, bastard.
RALPH	Four more pints, pal.
ALL	THREE!
JUDD	Got any pork scratchings?
ERIC	Hey, watch me shirt.
RALPH	Look who's pushing?
LES	Packed in't it?
JUDD	Let me get to them bogs.
ERIC	Excuse me.
RALPH	Four pints.
ALL	FOUR!
JUDD	And a whisky, love, please.
ALL	FIVE!
ERIC	Excuse me, love.
LES	I gave you a fiver.
JUDD	Fat gett.
RALPH	Four pints, four bags of beef, four bags of salted peanuts and four whisky chasers.
ALL	(*thumbs*) Yeah! SIX! SEVEN!
JUDD	Have you got any cashews?
ERIC	Hey twat, I've been stood here a month.
LES	Can we have some service down here?

RALPH   I'm next, love.

ERIC   Shut your mouth, skullhead.

JUDD   I'm being served, love, thanks.

          (*The four lads recoil as they see beer spill all over*
          ERIC's [BAZ's] *trousers*.)

ERIC   Ooooooh! Look at that. Somebody's spilt beer all
          over my suit.

JUDD   Daft gett.

ERIC   It's brand new.

LES   It'll dry.

JUDD   How many have we had?

RALPH   Ten.

JUDD   Time for another.

ERIC   I've only had nine.

RALPH   Are we off?

ERIC   D'you think we'll get in?

JUDD   Should do.

LES   Hope there's no trouble.

ERIC   There's four of us.

ALL   Yeah.

RALPH   Come on. Let's get down there, pick something up.

ALL   Right.

ERIC   Hang on.

LES   What?

ERIC   Piss call.

ALL   Oh yeah.

(They all turn their backs as if peeing and then turn back to face the audience.)

JUDD   We'd better split up.

LES   Why?

JUDD   The Bouncers.

ERIC   Don't let you in. In groups.

RALPH   Ok. Me and Kev. Right.

JUDD   Yeah. And me and . . . *(Realising who he's paired off with.)* Oh bollocks!

(Just as they are about to move away they all freeze. Pause. They once more become the girls we saw earlier in the hairdresser sequence. ERIC [MAUREEN], LES [ROSIE], JUDD [ELAINE], and RALPH [SUZY] all stand together in a circle having a laugh and a drink in a pub. They are all dressed up in their brand new clothes ready for the night out. This should be communicated to the audience through their actions. They introduce themselves one by one.)

ERIC   Maureen. Massive but nice. Fat but cuddly. Not a bag, but likes a drink and a laugh. A bit busty. *(Silly laugh.)*

LES   Rosie. Birthday today. Tall and slim, hair all permed. I had it done at Barbara's.

ERIC   It's nice. It really suits you.

LES   Thank you.

ERIC   Cow.

LES   I've had a drink. I feel a bit tiddly. Hey, it will end in tears. Hello luv.

ERIC   Hello.

LES	Have you lost a bit of weight?
JUDD	Plain Elaine.
ERIC/ LES	It's a shame.
JUDD	Left school at sixteen with one GCSE in metalwork. I'm on the dole.
ERIC/ LES	It's such a shame.
JUDD	Enjoys a good night out but doesn't expect to get picked up though. Handy in a fight . . . come here ya bastard. Hiya.
ERIC/ LES	Hiya.
RALPH	Rose, Maureen, Elaine . . . Hiya.
ALL	Hiya Suzy.
RALPH	Sexy . . . I've got stockings on under my dress. Do you wanna look? You cheeky getts! Go on then. Anybody's for half a lager. Goes under the sunbed . . brown all over. I bet you would fancy it, big boy. Ooh, he's nice that one. Is that your head or has your neck thrown up?
LES	I'll say he is. Yeah. Right. Who wants what?
JUDD	I'll have a pint of Guinness . . . no, only a joke. I'll have a brandy and lime.
ERIC	Well. I'll have a lager and black because if I have any more I'll be on my back.
LES	As usual.
ERIC	You cheeky sod.
LES	Sorry.

RALPH   I'll have a Piña Colada.

ERIC   Christ. Listen to her.

RALPH   Well I'm eighteen.

LES   She doesn't bloody care. I feel a bit sick.

ERIC   You'll be alright when we get down there.

LES   Are we getting the bus?

RALPH   Well, I'm not walking it in these shoes.

ALL   They're lovely.

RALPH   I know.

JUDD   I'm gonna put a record on.

ALL   Ya da da da da da da ya da da da da.

          (JUDD *walks up to an imaginary juke box,
          represented by* ERIC. LES *and* RALPH *join* JUDD
          around the juke box.)

RALPH   Put that on 3A. I like that.

JUDD   No. It's crap.

LES   I think you should put *Wham* on.

JUDD   I'm putting on a funky disco record.

RALPH   I'm afraid you are not, because I like this one here
          by *Bros*. (*Repeats as if the record is sticking.*)

ALL   When will I be famous?

          (*Sudden blackout and freeze. The actors walk to the
          side of the stage. A dark and foreboding sound
          filters out from the speakers. The pace has been fast
          and hectic up until this point, but now the stage is
          quite still. We are outside the club. Eerie,
          disturbing music plays as we move into a mime
          sequence during which the bouncers come to life.*)

*During this sequence each actor should create and
display a kind of larger-than-life character for each
bouncer. It is at this point that the individual
characteristics of each bouncer are established.
Ordinary mannerisms and gestures are grotesquely
exaggerated as one by one, the bouncers step
forward to introduce themselves through mime.
JUDD, for example, walks slowly and cautiously to
the centre of the stage, looks around, takes a hand
exerciser out of his pocket and begins to do a series
of exercises. He does so to the point of exhaustion,
his face grimacing as the seeping pain of lactic acid
invades his forearm muscles. He puts away the
exerciser and has a moment's silence to himself. He
takes a comb out of his pocket and begins to
carefully comb his hair. When he has completed this
highly meticulous activity he puts the comb away
and enjoys another moment's contemplation. He
spits on the floor, rubs the spit into the ground with
his foot and then cracks his knuckles. All these
actions are executed with the greatest attention to
detail and are outrageously heightened as indicated
above. Once JUDD has finished his sequence, RALPH
moves centre stage and repeats the ritual. Once
finished, he stands by JUDD. LES joins them, once
more enacting the ritual. Finally they speak. Each
word is delivered with much more emphasis than
would appear necessary as they acknowledge each
other.)*

LES   Judd?

JUDD   Les.

RALPH   Les?

LES   Ralph.

RALPH   Judd?

JUDD   Ralph.

             (LUCKY ERIC *joins the group.*)

ERIC   Ralph?

RALPH   Lucky Eric.

JUDD   Eric?

ERIC   Judd, Les.

LES   Lucky Eric. Alright?

ERIC   Yeah. Why?

LES   Cold innit?

RALPH   Yeh. Bitter.

JUDD   Any trouble last night?

LES   Usual. Couple of punks got glassed.

JUDD   Nothing special then?

RALPH   No.

LES   I wanted to have 'em, but Eric said no.

ERIC   You're too violent, Les. You can't control yourself.

LES   You don't have any fun, Eric. That's your trouble. Gerrin' past it.

ERIC   (*totally manic*) Don't you ever say that I am getting past it! Ever! (*Moves to* LES.)

JUDD   Many in?

RALPH   Packed. Early rush, then it'll tail off.

ERIC   That's Fridays for you.

JUDD   I got a basket meal for nothing yesterday.

ERIC   When?

JUDD   Yesterday.

LES   Who gave it to you?

JUDD   That girl.

ERIC	Oh yeah?
RALPH	Nice one she is, nice tea bag.
JUDD	Not bad.
ERIC	Yeah, all right in the dark.
RALPH	A bit fat around the buttocks if you ask me.
ERIC	Sommat to grab innit?
JUDD	Chicken it was. Tender.
LES	And chips?
JUDD	No chips. Fattening!
ERIC	Short legs.
RALPH	Yeah right.
ERIC	Optical illusion, that is.
JUDD	What? That chips are fattening?
RALPH	How come?
ERIC	Makes her arse look bigger.
LES	Nearer to the ground.
RALPH	Good centre of gravity, chickens.
ERIC	How's the judo?
RALPH	Not bad thanks.
ERIC	Still training?
RALPH	Yeah, twice a week. And you?
JUDD	Couldn't train hamsters.
ERIC	I trained you though, didn't I?
JUDD	Didn't train the wife too well though, did you rubber gob?

ERIC   Leave my wife out of it you.

JUDD   I hear she's putting it about a bit.

ERIC   Don't believe all you hear Judd, your head'll blow up.

JUDD   I know a bloke who says he's had her.

LES   Leave it Judd.

ERIC   I could have you any time.

JUDD   The king is dead, Eric.

ERIC   Every day I go powerlifting, get the hate out of my body, squeeze the pain out of my chest. I bench pressed three hundred and fifty four pounds yesterday.

JUDD   Who?

ERIC   Me.

LES   When?

ERIC   Yesterday.

LES   Get pillocked.

ERIC   No pillock doubting Thomas, no pillock.

JUDD   You couldn't press a button.

ERIC   Could have done two reps.

JUDD   Three hundred and fifty four pounds, that's er . . . fifteen pounds in a stone? Eight stones in a kilo?

RALPH   That's heavy, Judd.

ERIC   What can you bench Judd?

JUDD   Something.

ERIC   Still wrestling?

JUDD   No.

LES   Still on the dole aren't you?

JUDD   No.

RALPH   Doing a bit of nicking?

JUDD   No. Well a bit.

ERIC   It's a bit quiet out here tonight, isn't it . . . too quiet.

RALPH   It'll soon liven up when the pubs turn out. They'll all be streaming down here, like sheep.

ALL   (*chanting*) Here we go, here we go, here we go. (*As if downing another pint.*) FOURTEEN!

RALPH   Bastards!

ERIC   What time is it?

JUDD   Well, the big hand is on nine . . .

LES   Early doors yet. No need to start gerrin' aggressive.

RALPH   Yes, they'll all be coming down here, looking for a woman.

LES   Yeah, a big buxom woman.

JUDD   Or a small petite woman.

ERIC   Or a bloke.

JUDD   Yes, there's usually one or two of them about and all.

ERIC   Is there?

LES   They're all right you know really.

RALPH   No, they are not all right you know really.

LES   They are . . . they are the same as us. They've got the same feelings, the same sex drives.

ERIC   Have they, Leslie?

LES   Yes they have, 'cos one of my best mates . . .

RALPH   Hold on a minute, Les.

ERIC   What are you on about Les?

LES   Now listen. I was just about to say . . .

RALPH   Yes . . .

LES   That one of my best mates . . .

RALPH   Yes . . .

LES   Once knew a fella who once and only once, worked in a club for gay people.

RALPH   Tell us another one.

ERIC   You can't be too careful these days, Les.

RALPH   Each to their own. That's it. Each to their bloody own. You have just got to let people get on with what they want . . . that is my philosophy for life.

ERIC   Fair enough Ralph. Fair enough. I like to hear a man express his philosophy. Fair enough. (*Pause.*) You can borrow my handbag any night, sweetie.

RALPH   Steady on.

ERIC   Yeah?

RALPH   Steady on.

ERIC   Or what?

RALPH   Are we trying to start something, Eric?

ERIC   Could be.

RALPH   Are we trying to encourage a conflict situation?

ERIC   Might be, Mr Inner Calm.

            (RALPH *takes up a strong stance and invites* ERIC *to
            hit him.*)

RALPH   Come on then . . . there . . . now . . .

            (ERIC *makes a move as if to hit him, but stops. It is a
            hoax.* ERIC *stands and laughs at* RALPH. *The other
            bouncers see the latent danger but as this is a
            regular occurrence, they are not unduly disturbed.*)

RALPH   Powerlifters. I've shit 'em.

ERIC   Judo. Puffballs.

            (*They back off. There is a moment's quiet.*)

JUDD   Eric, Eric . . . Remember that Rugby Union trip that
            came down.

LES   Zulu warriors?

RALPH   None of that tonight, I hope.

JUDD   Caused chaos.

ERIC   Bloody idiots.

LES   College boys.

ALL   (*sing*) She's a rag shag-a-bag, she's an automatic
            whore.

JUDD   Chuff heads.

RALPH   College, my arse.

LES   They came down here doing their college antics,
            hitting each other over the head with beer trays,
            dropping their trousers every five minutes.

JUDD   Like I said, one or two of them about.

RALPH   Animals.

JUDD   They have these special nights, you know. Rugby clubs. Sex and all that; live.

LES   Yeah?

JUDD   I thought of joining.

ERIC   I was just thinking.

JUDD   What with?

ERIC   My brain, Judd, up here. Where you keep budgie food and dubbin. I've got a brain.

JUDD   You ought to be on Mastermind, Eric, if you've got a brain. Fancy having a brain and doing this job. At this rate you're going to end up on Krypton Factor or sommat.

ERIC   And at this rate you're going to end up on a life support, Judd.

LES   Leave it out, Eric.

RALPH   You're very tetchy, Eric.

ERIC   Oh yeah?

RALPH   Yes. You're very very tetchy.

LES   What were you thinking about, Eric, with this brain that you've got?

ERIC   I was just thinking: women.

LES   Oh yeah, and what about them?

ERIC   They're weird!

LES   They're not as weird as having a beard up your arse.

RALPH   What on earth are you trying to say, Eric?

ERIC   Different attractions. Strange.

JUDD   What's strange about women?

ERIC   They laugh at you when you're naked.

ALL   Oh yeah.

RALPH   I was just thinking as well. I mean, where is
            everybody? I'm freezing to bloody death out here.
            Why's that?

JUDD   Because it's cold.

RALPH   Because nobody's turned up yet, so let me get me
            hands on somebody, warm them up a bit.

JUDD   They'll all be gerrin' some beer down their bloody
            necks, stood about in plush pubs, slopping beer
            down 'em. Either that or they're watching the
            bloody telly, come down here about half eleven,
            tight-fisted sods.

LES   It's still early.

RALPH   I'm going inside in a minute.

            (ERIC *has been gazing into the night.*)

ERIC   Look at them lights, look at all those lights.

JUDD   'The City by Night', by Lucky Eric, 'an artist's
            impression'.

LES   Piss artist.

ERIC   Them lights are like people, just like people's lives.

LES   What's he on about?

ERIC   Them flats, people live in them flats.

JUDD   He's a bloody genius, you know.

ERIC   Couples, huddled together in one or two rooms.

RALPH   Mom, mom, the rent man's here.

LES   Show him to the bedroom love.

ERIC   Carrying out relationships.

JUDD   Aye eye, here we go. Getting round to sex.

ALL   NO NO NO . . . YES!

ERIC   In them flats, somebody'll be having a shag right
        now.

        (*Pause, while the idea sinks in.*)

LES   Lucky bastards . . .

ERIC   All over the world people will be dying, and
        conceiving children and growing vegetables and
        shagging.

LES   Lucky bastards.

RALPH   Don't let it get to you, Eric.

LES   Don't get depressed.

ERIC   And we're stood here out in the cold like four daft
        pricks.

LES/
RALPH/ (*shouting*) Lucky Eric's first speech!
JUDD

        (*The three bouncers fade into the background as the
        lights dim and a spotlight comes up on* ERIC. *He
        delivers his speech with total sincerity.*)

ERIC   The girls are young; some look younger than the
        others. It worries me. It does. I'm not thick. You
        think that we're thick. We're not. I'm not. Got to be
        eighteen. I turn a blind eye. We live by rules but we
        all turn blind eyes. I don't know whether or not it's
        a good thing . . . still at school half of them; they
        come down here Friday, Saturday, saving up all
        week the money they've earned working part-time
        in the supermarket. What else is there? With their
        made-up faces, floating about on a cloud of *Estee
        Lauder*, wearing *Impulse* and footless tights, or
        flashing wrinkle-free flesh, of schoolgirl knicker
        dreams, flesh of sunburnt leg; hairless leg, shapely,

untouched by human hand, leg. I sweat a lot.
Wouldn't you? Two drinks and they're going; legs
opening to any particular denizen of the night with
car keys and *Aramis* splashed face, maybe even *Old
Spice*; drunken, free, giddy, silly girls, wanting to
be women, done too soon. Vulnerable, cruel world
the morning after, or the month after when the curse
hasn't taken its spell! I wanna touch them, squeeze
them, keep them safe. Smell like Pomander, a
lingering smell. Pure and dirty, innocent and vulgar;
it all withers, washes away. Eighteen going on
thirty-five, because they think they've got to,
because they're forced to . . . I dunno.

(*Lights come up and the other bouncers take up
their positions and start to talk once more - all as if
the speech had never occurred.*)

JUDD   Ever have any strange sex, Leslie?

LES   No. Never.

RALPH   I have. I've had some of that.

LES   Yeah? What was it like?

RALPH   Strange.

ERIC   I nearly had chinky once.

JUDD   Oh yeah. Army, was it?

ALL   Shun . . .

RALPH   In Malaya, was it?

          (*They all make Malaya noises.*)

ERIC   No . . . Fish and chip shop down Blenheim Terrace.
          Nice woman; didn't understand a word she said
          though.

LES   That the language of love, Eric?

JUDD   Number 34 with rice, eh?

RALPH   Sixty-nine, knowing Lucky Eric.

        (*They all laugh manically.*)

ERIC   Couldn't go through with it.

JUDD   Why?

ERIC   Married.

LES   He's crazy.

JUDD   I'm in the mood tonight.

RALPH   Tell us something new.

JUDD   I could shag a rat.

RALPH   The power of the spoken word.

        (*Lights change, music booms. We are in the disco.
        RALPH is the DJ. He speaks nonsense down the
        microphone. We only catch a few words. Then he
        begins the following speech in a spotlight.*)

RALPH   Hope that you're all having a greeeaaat time down
        here at *Mr Cinders*. Remember that on Tuesday, yes
        that's Tuesday of next week, we'll be having a
        video special. Do do come along and enjoy that
        extravaganza. I shall be giving away a few bottles
        of champagne very shortly for a number of people
        who are celebrating their twenty-first today; key of
        the door and, let's hope, key of another special
        place. Are there any nymphomaniacs down here this
        evening? Yes, there are. Well, I'll be playing
        something for you very soon, and it will not be a
        record. Okay, okay, let's just stop the music for a
        moment and put up your hand, yes put up your hand
        if you are a virgin. I don't believe it, ladies and
        gentleman, there are no virgins down here this
        evening. Looks like it's going to be a night to
        remember. This is Shalamar . . .

        (*The music plays loudly. The four actors now
        become ELAINE, ROSIE, SUZY and MAUREEN. They pick
        up their handbags and walk with great dignity into*

*the middle of the dance floor. They then all place
their handbags in a pile on the floor and begin to
dance around the bags to the music.)*

ALL   (*with the song*) 'Gonna Make This a Night to
             Remember'.

ERIC   Maureen - short but nice, fat but sickly.

LES   Rosie - feels a bit tiddly.

JUDD   Elaine - sweating like a race horse, wants to sit
             down.

RALPH   Suzy - sexy and flashing it about a bit.

JUDD   Christ, I'm sweating.

LES   Ya what?

JUDD   I'm dripping.

RALPH   I am.

ERIC   I feel sick . . .

RALPH   You what?

ERIC   I feel sick.

LES   It's too warm.

JUDD   Ya what Rosie?

LES   I feel dizzy.

JUDD/   Happy birthday.
RALPH

LES   Shut up.

ERIC   I think I'm gonna spew.

JUDD   Oh isn't she pathetic?

ERIC   Let me get to the toilet.

LES   What's she had?

RALPH   Five barley wines.

ERIC   Hang on a minute. I feel all right now, it was just indigestion.

JUDD   (*to the audience*) And then, as if by magic, the drunken tears, and Rosie discovers twenty-firsts are not all fun . . .

ERIC   Her boyfriend Patrick is seen kissing another . . .

RALPH   With several large shorts imbibed, the tears and mascara begin to run.

LES   He's left me for another, over in a dark corner snogging, and French kissing, tongue job to say the least. I feel myself get all angry and upset inside but I've already had enough drinks to fill a bath. The hate turns inside to self-pity and the tears begin to flow and with it the mascara. And soon my face looks like a miner's back in the showers, rivulets of black *Max Factor*. And then the friends . . .

ALL   That's us.

LES   . . . begin to comfort me and offer me advice on how and what to do.

JUDD   Burn her face off.

LES   Oh don't be daft, Elaine.

ERIC   Castrate the philanderer.

RALPH   Get your LPs back.

LES   Then the plague begins to spread, the tears begin to flow and all advice becomes sobbing woe. Look at him sitting there as cool as a cucumber. I've been going out with him for two days . . . it's pathetic.

ALL   Pathetic, pathetic, pathetic . . .

(*Loud music comes up.*)

RALPH   I love this. I've gorra dance.

ERIC   Ooooooooh, it goes right through me.

RALPH   It goes right through me an' all.

LES   What hasn't?

RALPH   I heard that, Rosie.

LES   I'm sorry, Sue.

RALPH   You are not coming to Benidorm.

ALL   (*with song*) Ooh wee . . .

           (*Lights change and we are suddenly outside the club
           once more.* ERIC *and* JUDD *are the two bouncers,
           patrolling the doors.* RALPH *and* LES *play a variety
           of characters trying to enter the club.*)

ERIC   Seems to be going quite steady Judd.

JUDD   Twenty nine stones.

ERIC   What?

JUDD   Twenty nine stones.

ERIC   What is?

JUDD   Three hundred and fifty four pounds. It's heavy that
           is Eric, it's twenty-nine stones.

ERIC   Right.

JUDD   I could bench that.

ERIC   Don't start.

JUDD   I could beat you any day. I'll have you now.

ERIC   Don't.

JUDD   I've shit bigger turds than you.

ERIC   Leave it.

JUDD Arm wrestle.

ERIC No.

JUDD You're soft.

ERIC Leave it Judd, just leave it.

JUDD The King is dead Eric.

  (*Enter* WAK *and* WAK *downstage.*)

RALPH Wak.

LES And Wak, all dressed up very smart.

RALPH But we look a bit rough.

BOTH Hey come ed come ed.

ERIC Evening fellas.

BOTH Evening.

JUDD Where are you from?

LES About.

JUDD Oh yeah?

ERIC Not from round about here though are you?

RALPH Not from round about here no.

ERIC Oh.

LES Is there a problem like?

JUDD No, no problem.

LES Great, we're in, come on.

ERIC Are you cut sort of celebrating like?

RALPH Yeah, you could say that.

LES Yeah, we're celebrating, yeah.

ERIC	What, a stag night is it, lads?
LES	Yeah that's right, a stag night.
JUDD	Sorry lads, can't let you in.
RALPH	Why?
ERIC	No stag parties allowed in.
LES	You what?
ERIC	You heard.
RALPH	Jesus Christ.
JUDD	Sorry fellas, but rules is rules.
RALPH/ LES	Please.
ERIC	Go away.
RALPH/ LES	Come ed, come ed, come ed.
ERIC	Soft bastards.
JUDD	Always works.
ERIC	Stag nights; it's always a good laugh.
JUDD	No wonder they're losing custom in here.
	(RALPH *and* LES *enter again, this time as punks. They spread their hands above their heads to create spiky hair, spit, spew, pogo, etc.*)
JUDD	Where are you punks going?
LES	In the discotheque, man.
ERIC	Not dressed like that you're not. Go home and change your tutu.
RALPH	Hey man don't mess with my tutu.

ERIC   Don't call me man . . . forkhead.

RALPH   Come on man, we're not going to cause any trouble in there. (*He spits.*)

JUDD   I know you're not 'cos I'm not going to let you in. (*He spits on* RALPH.)

RALPH   Hey did you see that?

LES   Yes I did, and I think it was a very good shot . . . come on, let's go and have a pint of piss in the cesspit . . .

RALPH   Hey Ruffage.

LES   Yes Ashley.

RALPH   Do you know what they are . . . ? They are fascist pigs . . . they've spoilt the whole evening and I am shortly intending to write a song about the experience.

LES   Go on then.

RALPH   Fascist pigs.

LES   Fascist pigs.

RALPH   (*singing*) Oh you fascist pigs . . .

LES   (*singing*) Oh you fascist pigs . . .

RALPH   What do you think of that then?

LES   They're lovely lyrics.

(LES *and* RALPH *pogo off upstage. The actors suddenly change position so that* ERIC *and* JUDD *become the lads,* TERRY *and* BAZ, *and* RALPH *and* LES *become bouncers once more.*)

ERIC/   (*chanting*) Here we go, here we go, here we go . . .
JUDD

ERIC   Watch these two, Terry.

JUDD   Why's that, Baz?

ERIC   Might be a bit awkward.

RALPH   Evening, lads.

ERIC   Evening.

LES   Are you members?

JUDD   You what?

RALPH   Members only tonight, lads, sorry.

JUDD   It wasn't members only last night.

ERIC   Or last Friday. Play the game, fellas.

RALPH   Only pillocking, lads. In you come. Thirty eight
          quid each.

JUDD   You what? Hear that, Baz?

ERIC   It's only thirty bob.

LES   Let them in, Ralph.

RALPH   You're in. Urine?

          (ERIC *and* JUDD *enter the club, and walk upstage.*)

RALPH   Why did you let them in?

LES   I'm going to do that fat one.

RALPH   You're weird, Les.

LES   Oh yeah.

RALPH   With the greatest respect you're very weird.

LES   I know.

          (*They all now become the lads.*)

RALPH   Baz-

JUDD Terry-

RALPH Jerry-

LES Kev-

(*They all take another imaginary pint and slop it down.*)

ALL SIXTEEN! And a vindaloo!

LES In the toilets

ERIC   Lav

RALPH   Bog

JUDD   Shit house!

(*Standing upstage centre, they are in the club toilets. Each of them passes wind and there is a delight of visual scatological jokes. Finally, they are ready to urinate. LES narrates, conveying the atmosphere whilst the others act out the situation.*)

LES At about twelve o'clock, the toilets are the hell-hole of the disco. Keeping your feet on the slippery tiled floor is a feat in itself. Many an aff-air has been ruined by loose footing; one quick slip and you're up to your hip in urine.

(*One of the actors slips and drowns.*)

When you actually reach the urinals, your Hush Puppies are soaking, seeping through to your socks. In the urinals, there is by this time a liberal smattering of tab ends, and the odd soupçon of sick. In the sink there's probably a Durex packet, with the condoms still inside, some forgetful stud having left them. The smell is nauseous; you stand holding your breath trying to pee, reading the wall, trying your best not to catch anyone's eye.

ERIC (*reading*) You don't come here to mess about to have a piss . . . oh, charming . . .

JUDD   (*reading*) Follow this line . . . (*He follows a line, moving slowly.*) You are now pissing on your foot.

ERIC   Rearrange this well-known phrase. Shit Mrs Thatcher is a . . .

RALPH   I've got it! Mrs Shit is a Thatcher.

JUDD   Don't be stupid. It's . . . Shit Thatcher, Mrs is a . . .

LES   Here's one; save water, piss on a friend.

(*They start to look at one another's genitals.*)

ERIC   (*to* RALPH) What the hell is that?

RALPH   It's mine.

ERIC   Jesus Christ!

JUDD   What's up?

ERIC   Look at that.

JUDD   Bloody hell.

RALPH   What's the matter with you lot?

ERIC   (*to* LES) Hey, seen this?

LES   What?

ERIC   Look at that I've never seen one so big.

LES   Bleeding hell.

RALPH   Haven't you seen one before?

ERIC   It's like a baby's arm with an orange in its fist.

RALPH   Let's have a look at yours then?

ERIC   Gerra way you pervert.

JUDD   It's not natural.

LES   It's an offensive weapon is that, he could mug somebody with it.

RALPH   Oh yeah?

LES   Come on let's get back on the dance floor.

(They all zip up their trousers. RALPH has buttons.)

ERIC   Do you fancy a bit of a laugh?

ALL   Yeah . . . *(Laughter.)*

(Music: Carmina Burana. Suddenly they are bouncers once more.)

LES   Are we going inside or what?

RALPH   Eager tonight Les?

LES   I want to watch the skirt. I wanna see all them buttocks, shit I wanna talk to 'em.

RALPH   You want to talk to some buttocks?

JUDD   He'll talk to anything.

LES   Just what do you say to women in here? How do you chat 'em up?

RALPH   You just start talking to them an opening gambit.

LES   Like what?

JUDD   Shut up and get your tits out?

LES   Subtle.

RALPH   Something like that.

LES   Mind you this is better than over twenty-fives night.

RALPH   The floor boards creak and out come the creeps.

LES   Dripping in wall to wall cellulite.

JUDD   Eric's favourite.

RALPH	Over twenty-fives night?
LES	Grab a granny night.
JUDD	He's looking for a women aren't you Eric?
ERIC	Shut up you.
JUDD	Can't keep one when he's got one, doesn't know how to treat them. I think I saw your ex-wife down here on Tuesday, Eric.
RALPH	Leave it Judd.
JUDD	And she wasn't alone.
ERIC	Shuddup.
JUDD	With a couple of young blokes I think.
LES	Judd leave it.
ERIC	I'll have you.
JUDD	Oh yeah?
RALPH	Leave it.
JUDD	No.
ERIC	I will have you Judd.
JUDD	I don't think so.
ERIC	I will.
JUDD	Come on then.
ERIC	Don't set me off.
JUDD	Come on.
ERIC	Don't Judd. Just don't.
	(*Silence.*)
ALL	Lucky Eric's second speech.

ERIC   On Tuesdays it's over twenty-fives night. Mutton dressed as lamb night, mutton dressed as anything night. Sad Night. And you can see the baggage they're bringing, husband dead, wife left him, divorced, run off, left him for the milkman. Or the businessman with a night to kill and a face full of lager. Skin bursting at the seams with alcohol, desperate for an illicit fling before returning to the wife to speak of a dull night in Wakefield, nothing to do, "Yes dear, went to bed at half ten." And the fire doors tell their secret stories. Used prophylactics, tons of them, a mountain of condoms and pitta bread behind the disco. Durex lay like dead Smurfs, a symbol of a battle won, a conquest taken, another victory against a hairdresser from Garforth. And the pissed-up pale-faced lager lousy lager louts strut their funky stuff, attempting to pick up something twice their age, for fun? For a laugh? And the skeletons of their pasts float away, drunk on a mixture of sweat and Southern Comfort. And she's there, the wife is there, the ex-wife is there. In the hunt, on the dance floor, moving awkwardly amongst the anarchy they call dancing. And the pissed up pale face, chats to her, touches her. I wish they'd start it with me, I wish they'd start something with me. I wish one of those skinny balmy bastards would just start it with me. Just start it with me. Just let them start it with me . . .

(ERIC *is near to breakdown. The other bouncers watch him with some glee. Music plays. Slowly* JUDD, LES *and* RALPH *exit. The spotlight fades on* ERIC.)

Interval.

ACT TWO

RALPH, JUDD *and* LES *enter and form a line, centre stage.*
LUCKY ERIC *joins the line, inspecting the audience.*

JUDD   (*to audience*) What are you laughing at?

ERIC   Do you think they're ready for it?

LES   No. But they're gonna get it.

          (*Loud disco music plays.* RALPH *becomes the DJ
          once again. The others become the lads, by now
          fairly drunk, attempting to dance whilst the DJ
          speaks.*)

RALPH   Yeah! Wow! Things are really happening down here
          tonight. Have some fun, yeah have some fun. Tell
          you what girls . . . tell you what we'll do . . . the
          first girl who brings me a matching pair of bra and
          knickers, yes a pair of knickers and a bra, there'll
          be a bottle of Asti Spumante and a fortnight's free
          entry, get it, entry, to *Mr Cinders*. So come on girls,
          get them off and bring them up to me, marvellous
          Michael Dee, the DJ with the big B . . . (*Back
          outside.*) I think that the snot up my nose is frozen.

ERIC   Very interesting.

RALPH   Aren't you cold?

ERIC   No, I've got blood in my veins, not water.

JUDD   All fat, that's why.

ERIC   Listen what's talking.

JUDD   That's muscle.

ERIC   That's shit.

RALPH   That's enough.

ERIC   Roll on two o'clock.

JUDD   Have we got any films in?

LES   Yeah. A bluey; it'll make your nose run, it's that blue.

JUDD   Where did you get it?

ALL   Video shop.

(Scene changes to the video shop. ERIC and RALPH are looking for videos. JUDD plays the shop assistant.)

LES   Have you got any of them video nasties?

JUDD   No, no, no, no . . . YES.

LES   Oh . . . what have you got?

JUDD   I've got 'Rambo One', 'Rambo Two', 'Rambo Three' to thirty-seven, 'Friday the Thirteenth', 'Friday the Fifteenth', 'Monday the Twenty-third', 'October the Ninth', 'My Mother's Birthday', 'Bank Holiday Sunday' and most of the Religious Holidays in 3-D.

RALPH   Queen Kong, the story of a sixty-four foot gay gorilla.

LES   Yes that's it, something a bit blue.

JUDD   I've got light blue, dark blue, sky blue, and navy blue.

LES   Navy blue?

JUDD   Or something with animals . . .

(They all grunt and gurgle like animals.)

LES   I'll take the one with animals. The boys should enjoy this.

(Back outside the club.)

ERIC   Perverts . . .

JUDD   At two o'clock the disco shuts . . . free drinks all
          round.

LES   At least we've got a video now.

RALPH   Yeah, you can say that again.

LES   At least we've got a video now.

JUDD   Which beats the old projector we used to have,
          three-quarters of an hour fixing up the bloody
          projector. Then with sweaty hand in tight polyester,
          we'd watch the twitchin' and the screamin'. Like
          fish in a barrel, we'd fidget and jump watching plot
          and orifice explored.

          (*All the bouncers have a drink. They then mime
          setting up the projector, ready to watch the blue
          movie.* RALPH *and* ERIC *act out the film.* ERIC *plays a
          buxom Swede taking her clothes off, about to have a
          shower.* RALPH *plays the postman. Sleazy
          background music and strobe lights should give the
          scene a cinematic feel. The other bouncers provide
          a commentary.*)

RALPH   (*as though the doorbell*) Bing bong . . .

ERIC   Whom de iz eet?

RALPH   It ist me. Nobby, ze Swedish postmant . . .

LES   Hey up. It's Nobby, Swedish postman.

ERIC   Come on ze in, Nobby. I'm unt der shopwer, unt . . .

LES   (*excitedly*) Go on, Nobby lad . . .

RALPH   Ver ist der usband?

ERIC   Engagedist unt ont dert buziness . . .

LES   Husband away on business . . .

JUDD   Go on, Nob!

ERIC   I am zo lonely wit my usband in Oslo . . .

LES   Aye, aye . . . she's lonely with her husband away on
         business in Oslo. I can understand that. Can you
         Judd? A women alone and all that.

JUDD   Gerron with the film.

ERIC   Oh. I've dropped the soapen on the flooren.

RALPH   She's dropped the soapen on the flooren.

LES   She's dropped the soap.

JUDD   Go on . . . Nobby, my son . . .

         (*As* NOBBY [ERIC] *is about to move the action freezes
         as if the film has jammed. Strobe stops.*)

JUDD   Give that projector a boot.

ALL   Boot!

         (*Strobe re-starts. The action is now played in
         reverse, as though the film is being rewound, up to
         the doorbell ringing at the start. We snap out of this
         scene and the actors are all bouncers again.*)

JUDD   It's not fair.

ERIC   Porno films . . . a waste of time.

JUDD   It pays your wages.

LES   There's something wrong with a bloke who doesn't
         enjoy a good bluey, that's what I say.

RALPH   I think that's a fair comment, Les.

JUDD   Eric doesn't like them. He thinks it's degrading.

LES   What's degrading about it; they get paid for it. I
         mean it's not exactly as if they're doing it for
         peanuts.

JUDD   I'd do it for peanuts. I'd do it for one peanut . . .
         Eh? What a job? It's not exactly a matter of being a

good actor is it? Just get in there, get stripped off,
get stuck in . . . Not a bad job Eric, eh? Beats this
shit.

ERIC   You're an animal, Judd.

JUDD   Keep talking . . .

ERIC   An animal . . .

JUDD   How's that?

ERIC   Don't you know?

ALL   (*very softly*) Lucky Eric's third speech.

           (*As* ERIC *speaks, the others can act out the scene.
           Background music should play.*)

ERIC   I'm sat in this pub, just an ordinary pub, and it's
           Christmas. Everybody's had one over the eight. And
           there's a group of lads, football supporters, that
           type, eleven stone, walking about like they think
           they're Frank Bruno. And there's this girl nineteen,
           twenty, and she's drunk, and she's got it all there,
           the figure, the looks. The lads are laughing, joking
           with her. "Give us a kiss eh?" And she does. Well,
           it's Christmas, I think, well, it is Christmas. I sat
           watching for an hour. She was well pissed; they all
           had a go, kissing her, feeling her, lifting her skirt
           up. Nobody noticed, pub was packed. Merry
           Christmas they'd say, and line up for another kiss
           and a feel, each one going further than the other,
           until I could see the tops of her thighs bare. And in
           that pub, she had them all, or they had her, six of
           'em, in a pub. Nobody noticed, nobody noticed but
           me. It was a strange feeling, a weird feeling, I
           remember walking over to where they were. I was
           aroused more than ever before in my life. I'm so
           powerful, so powerful. I stood in front of them,
           looking at them. The first head was quite hard, but
           the others were soft, like eggs; they hit the wall and
           smashed. The girl stood up. "Give us a kiss," she
           said, "Give us a kiss." "Go home.", I said, "Please
           go home . . ."

(*Lights come up.*)

LES So what's the plan then?

JUDD Inside?

LES Yeah.

RALPH The usual.

LES What if there's a big fight, rush in, eh? Get some kicks in.

ERIC Don't be a twat all your life, Les. Have a night off.

LES A few kicks never hurt anybody.

JUDD Look at all those lights . . . them lights are like people . . . they are like people's lights . . .

ERIC Anybody could do this job.

LES Bollocks!

ERIC No they could, it's a matter of ego.

LES Isn't that Frankenstein's mate?

RALPH That's Igor.

LES Same innit?

ERIC His brain's painted on.

LES But he's handy though, Eric.

ERIC I'm telling you. It's all image.

RALPH Eric's got a point. I once heard some talk of a nightclub in Manchester that employed a woman.

JUDD Bollocks . . .

LES Pull the other one . . .

RALPH Straight up is this; she was a big fat woman.

JUDD   I know her.

RALPH   Whenever somebody was making an arsehole of
           themselves, she'd go over and tell 'em not to be so
           stupid, tell them to pull themselves together. She
           never had any trouble either.

JUDD   Can't see that happening down here; she'll probably
           get glassed.

LES   Or picked up.

ALL   HA HA HA.

           (*Inside the disco.* RALPH *becomes* SUZY, ERIC
           becomes BAZ, LES *becomes* KEV *and* JUDD *becomes*
           ELAINE.)

ERIC   It's ten past one. Baz is well gone.

LES   Kev is ready to try it on, with anyone with two legs
           and two tits. Two teeth, anything.

JUDD   Plain Elaine has got a pain in her head, she's ready
           for bed.

RALPH   Suzy is sexy, she's been flirting about.

ERIC   What about those two? Come on let's get in, have a
           bash.

LES   Just give a sec. I'm dying for a slash.

           (LES *moves off.* ERIC [BAZ] *now walks up to the
           girls.*)

ERIC   Now then girls, alright are we?

JUDD   Piss off fatty.

ERIC   You can't get around me that easy.

JUDD   You're ugly.

ERIC   That's nice What's your name?

RALPH   Suzy. I'm drunk you know?

ERIC   Wanna have a dance?

RALPH   What about my friend?

ERIC   I've got a mate, he's just gone for a slash, he'll be back in a dash. Come on shall we go . . .

JUDD   Hey, I hope I'm not gonna be left here?

RALPH   I'm only going for a dance, Elaine, that's all.

(ERIC *and* RALPH *move upstage as if to the dance floor and freeze.* LES *comes back from the toilet, and is faced with* JUDD [ELAINE].)

LES   Where's Baz?

JUDD   Is he fat?

LES   A bit.

JUDD   He's just got off with my friend.

LES   The lucky gett! Go on, pole it. He always gets the pretty ones.

JUDD   D'you wanna dance?

LES   Who me?

JUDD   Come on, I like you.

LES   Gerroff me.

(*Both couples now take up a smooching position. They begin to think aloud.*)

ERIC   God! She smells great, her chest's really warm. I can just about feel her arse. I think she's drunk. Oh no, I'm gerrin' a hard on. She's rubbin' herself against me.

(ERIC *moves his body in order to dance away from* RALPH [SUZY].)

RALPH   I don't know where I am, I'm sinking and spinning, round and round, round and round . . .

JUDD   So am I.

LES   This is bad news, I hope nobody sees me. I think Terry's drunk anyway. She's strong is this one. She's breaking my bleeding back. I just hope that she doesn't fall over. I can feel her fat.

JUDD   If he makes a move or tries anything with me I'll break his arms. He's nice and cute though, I'll say that much. I think he likes me . . .

LES   She is the ugliest girl I've ever met . . .

ERIC   I think I've pulled a cracker this time . . .

RALPH   I'll let him take me home but I'm not having sex.

ERIC   I bet she goes like a rabbit.

RALPH   I do.

LES   I hope she doesn't try and kiss me. I'll spew.

ERIC   Wait while I tell all the lads.

RALPH   His breath smells awful, I think he must smoke.

ERIC   Yes, I'm in here, no trouble.

RALPH   He's really too big, a bit of a joke. He's not what I'm after, not handsome and slim. I'll tell him I'm going to the loo, that should lose him . . . I'll have to nip to the toilet.

ERIC   You what?

RALPH   I've got to go to the toilet.

ERIC   What for?

RALPH   Don't be nosey.

ERIC   Don't be long, will yer?

RALPH   You wait here, don't move. I'll be back in a tick.

ERIC   Right.

            (RALPH *walks away from* ERIC. ERIC *freezes as he looks at his watch.*)

LES   Listen.

JUDD   What?

LES   I'll have to go now.

JUDD   Why?

LES   I should have turned into a pumpkin ten minutes ago.

JUDD   Oh yeah.

LES   Look can you let me go please . . .

JUDD   Give me a kiss first . . .

LES   I can't.

JUDD   Why?

LES   I've got something that I don't want you to catch.

JUDD   What's that?

LES   Me. I've got a terminal disease.

JUDD   You haven't. You're only saying that.

LES   Like fuck I am.

JUDD   You're stopping here with me, or I'll chop your face off.

LES   Look get off me you fat overweight disgusting horrible smelly fat slag.

(Music plays. "Feed The World". Slowly JUDD *exits. As he does* RALPH, *furious, comes to* LES.)

RALPH   Hey shit-breath, what have you been saying about our lass.

LES   I haven't been saying anything.

RALPH   You have . . . I heard you at the bar.

LES   Look twat, don't start. There's three of us.

RALPH   Don't start with me twat, there's three of us.

*(*RALPH *kicks* LES *in the bollocks. He falls.* JUDD *and* ERIC *enter. They stop the fight.)*

ALL   *(shout)* FIGHT!

(They all now dash to the centre of the stage, as bouncers and lads, grab each other and generally give the impression that there is a fight going on.)

ERIC   Come on you two. Leave it out. Get them out, Judd. Fire exit.

JUDD   Let's do the bastards.

ERIC   Let's just get them out.

JUDD   I'm going to do mine.

ERIC   Don't.

JUDD   Who are you talking to Eric?

ERIC   You, you daft bastard.

JUDD   Oh yeah.

RALPH   Hey no need to fight over us lads.

ERIC   Piss off . . . There's no need to do them over, just leave them. They're pissed up anyway.

JUDD   Who do you think you are, Eric?

ERIC   Nobody.

JUDD   You get up my back.

ERIC   Look, Judd, don't set me off.

JUDD   You weird bastard!

ERIC   I said, don't set me off.

JUDD   You shouldn't be doing this job. You should be bouncing at Mothercare. You're soft.

ERIC   Don't set me off.

JUDD   Soft inside.

ERIC   Don't set me . . .

JUDD   Soft bastard.

(ERIC *turns on* JUDD, *forces him to the ground and almost breaks his arm.* JUDD *lays prostrate,* LES *and* RALPH *run to the scene,* ERIC *makes a threat against the two of them.*)

ERIC   Come on, come on, I'll have you and all.

RALPH   Eric, it's me, it's Ralph, it's me.

ERIC   Sorry, Judd, sorry.

(JUDD *slowly gets to his feet and walks upstage with* LES. *Both of them speak together.*)

JUDD/   Lucky Eric's fourth and final speech.
LES

(*Spotlight on* ERIC.)

ERIC   We have these Miss Wet T-shirt and Miss Instring evenings. Eighteen year old beauties displaying their orbs through string vests or firm outlines on wet cotton, naked some of them, save their skimpy knickers. All of them somebody's daughters,

mothers some of them, my wife, one of them. And
the glossy polaroids on the doors outside show more
hideous topless antics. Breasts in beer glasses,
breasts smeared in shaving foam, breasts oiled and
on show. And Michael Dee the DJ, kisses and sucks
as if they were his own, slimy bastard. I see the
girls selling themselves for five minutes' fame. I
can see the staid state of exploitation, I can even
smell the peaches of their underarm roll-on. The
working class with no options left, exposing its
weakness. I feel very sad. I feel very protective, I
might pack it all in. I might pack it all in, fuck off
go home and listen to Elvis Presley.

(*Music plays. A spotlight picks out* RALPH *as
Michael Dee.*)

RALPH   Someone has just handed me a piece of paper from
          the dance floor and on it it asks me to dedicate this
          next record to Sharon and Darren who are out there
          getting it together. So tell him you love him Shaz,
          and tell her you love her, Davs. After all a little
          white lie never really hurt anyone did it . . . but
          let's be serious for a moment shall we. All of you
          girls out there tonight at *Mr Cinders*, later on when
          you're really getting it together spare a thought for
          me, and for our doormen, who couldn't even pull a
          muscle. And I know one of them who will certainly
          be going home, lonesome tonight.

ERIC   You're dead pal.

RALPH   Just a joke Eric, so remember me, Marvellous
          Michael Dee, your love doctor.

JUDD   Witch Doctor.

          (*Elvis plays: "Are You Lonesome Tonight"*. ERIC,
          JUDD, LES *sway*. RALPH *exits and enters upstage. The
          feel of a dream is conveyed.*)

LES   How's the wife Eric?

ERIC   Left me.

JUDD   How are the kids Eric?

ERIC   She took them with her.

LES   I hear she's seeing another bloke.

ERIC   He's in the Merchant Navy.

LES   Bit of a fat bastard.

JUDD   Yeh I know him.

RALPH   It's ten to two. Let's get back on the door.

LES   Yeh. Nothing left now, only the dogs.

RALPH   Coyote women.

LES   What?

RALPH   Coyote women. A women you take to bed tonight and love, but in the morning you see she's so ugly, and she's laid on your arm, that rather than wake her up you bite your own arm off. Coyote women.

LES   There's a lot of ugly men as well Ralph.

RALPH   Don't look at me when you say that.

JUDD   My arm hurts, I think he's broke my arm.

ERIC   I just sit in the flat waiting for the night time, waiting for the night to come around. Waiting for something to happen.

RALPH   Wanderlust.

LES   What is?

RALPH   That's why we're all here. Maybe tonight. Maybe this time we'll meet Sister Right. Maybe this time she'll be a nice girl? And it goes on and on. Wanderlust.

JUDD   My other arm's alright though.

ERIC   I'm just sat all day, in the dark, in the flat, in the cold, waiting, waiting for her, waiting for the kids, waiting for something to tell me I'm alive.

RALPH   Wanderlust.

JUDD   Let's go outside and nut some bastard.

        (*The bouncers howl like werewolves; "Three Times A Lady" can be heard. Suddenly we are in the disco with the lads.*)

RALPH   I was right you know?

ERIC   What d'you mean?

RALPH   There are only ugly 'uns left at two o'clock.

ERIC   I had one, but she walked off.

LES   Was she drunk?

JUDD   Must have been.

ERIC   Thanks.

LES   What about them four, over there?

RALPH   You what? She must weigh about seventeen stones.

ERIC   Better than nothing.

LES   She'd eat me.

JUDD   She'd eat us all.

ERIC   What do you say to someone that big?

LES   Sod off. You're big.

JUDD   Sod off, ya pig.

OTHERS No no no. He said big . . .

JUDD   Sod off ya big pig . . . it wasn't me that said that, it was me brother . . . and I haven't even got a brother . . .

LES You have, he's in *Star Trek* . . . You're right you
know, there are only scrag ends left at two o'clock.

JUDD Sod you lot, I'm game.

(LES *puts a paper bag on his head.*)

ALL And me.

(*The lads begin to dance with imaginary women.*)

RALPH Hey you don't sweat much for a big girl do you?

ERIC Can I borrow your face? I'm going ratting
tomorrow.

LES Do you want a drink? The bar's over there.

JUDD Give us a kiss, come on . . .

RALPH Didn't I used to go to school with you?

LES Does your Dad race pigeons . . . ?

ERIC Does your shit stink?

ALL Ooooooohhhh.

(*Slowly the lads change back to the bouncers. It is
closing time and the bouncers encourage people to
leave, see them off, etc.*)

ERIC Goodnight.

LES 'Night love, take care.

JUDD Goodnight.

RALPH 'Night . . .

ERIC Take it nice and steady.

LES (*looking at an imaginary woman*) Look at the
arsehole on that.

RALPH She's had a skinful . . .

JUDD   She's got handles on her hips.

(LES *becomes a punter, leaving the disco.*)

LES   I've had a great night, fellas . . . I've had a wonderful evening.

ERIC   Come away from him, mate.

LES   Does anyone know where I can get another bottle of champagne?

ERIC   You've had enough.

LES   Just one more bottle of champers, and everything will be tickety-tickety-boo.

JUDD   Tickety-tickety-fucking-boo. Watch this, I'll nut him.

ERIC   Leave him.

LES   Goodnight.

LES   (*as a bouncer*) Yeah goodnight, sir.

JUDD   Watch this, I'll nut him.

ERIC   Goodnight.

RALPH   Have a safe journey home.

(LES *becomes a bouncer once more.*)

LES   Goodnight. She's down here every night is that one.

JUDD   I thought I'd seen her before.

LES   She's been hanging around me like flies around shit.

ERIC   You said that Les, not us.

LES   I think she's after something.

RALPH   Eat shit, five million flies can't be wrong.

LES   What?

ERIC   Nice to hear that old one again. Goodnight, love.

ALL   Goodnight, goodnight, goodnight.

ERIC   And at two thirty around the back of the disco.

LES   You can hear the heavy breathing . . .

RALPH   The gasping and the sighing . . .

JUDD   The unzipping and the fumbling . . .

ERIC   And there she is, Sexy Suzy, having drunk a bathful of Bacardi, being felt and groped by a foul-mouthed tattooed coil of muscle from Leeds.

LES   And he tugs and fumbles and feels and fingers and pokes . . .

RALPH   And soaks her with sloppy kisses, the neck, the ears, the cleavage.

JUDD   And the elastic of her knickers snaps in the night, and he's inside her. Pumping.

LES   Groaning . . . Hard.

RALPH   Pushing, hard.

JUDD   Grabbing her hard.

LES   Loosing his footing on the asphalt.

ERIC   And Sexy Suzy, spins, and feels nothing, he pushes hard, gasping, scratching, sweating, and in her nothingness she eats a cold pizza. Delicately like a lady at a summer ball she picks at this Pizza Pepperoni.

RALPH   And he still pumps.

ERIC   And she still eats.

LES   And he still pumps and grasps, and slops kisses on her neck.

JUDD   And she still eats the pizza.

LES   And when he finally arrives, with a gasp of bad ale-
           smelling breath, a burp of an orgasm, he stands, legs
           shaking like a shitting dog, and he says . . .

JUDD   . . . that was fucking brilliant.

ERIC   And she finishes her feast, and discards the pizza
           box amongst the piles of condoms and pita bread.
           And don't tell us that it's not true, 'cos we've seen
           it, don't tell us that it's disgusting because we've
           smelt the awful stench. Don't tell us that it's all that
           they deserve, just tell us why . . . Tell us why?

           (*Suddenly* ERIC, JUDD, *and* RALPH *become the lads
           singing.*)

ALL   Here we go, here we go, here we go, here we go . . .

           (*Scene change to the lads now waiting for a taxi.*)

ERIC   Baz -

JUDD   Terry -

RALPH   Jerry -

LES   Kev -

ALL   Waaaaaaaaaaaaaay!

JUDD   Have you seen the length of this taxi queue? I'm
           friggin' freezin'.

LES   I wish I'd've put a big coat on.

RALPH   Oh no, look at that . . . I've got spew all over me
           shoe.

LES   I have.

JUDD   I have.

ERIC   I've got shit on mine.

ALL   Waaaaayyyy!

JUDD   Innit dark?

LES   Well it is half-past three.

JUDD   Half-past bloody three and we're stood out in the cold freezin' to bloody death.

ERIC   Just think, if I'd've got off with that Suzy I'd be in bed now snuggling up to her brown, tanned, sunburnt soft body.

ALL   Whaaaaaaaaaaaaaaay!

LES   Innit quiet? All asleep, and tucked away in their little boxes. Innit quiet? Listen, listen to the city. Quiet, innit? All those people asleep; It's like being in a painting.

JUDD   Is it bollocks.

ERIC   I'm dying for a slash.

RALPH   Do you feel pissed up.

JUDD   Who?

RALPH   You?

JUDD   (*considering the possibility*) No. Not now.

RALPH   No, I don't.

JUDD   I did about an hour ago. I've sobered up I think.

LES   It's the cold.

ERIC   I'm having a slash. (*He begins to urinate.*)

LES   (*pretending a taxi approaches*) TAXI!

ERIC   Oh shit! (*He attempts to do up his flies.*)

LES   Only a joke.

JUDD   I've spent thirty-five quid.

RALPH   Yeah?

JUDD   Jesus Christ, I've spent thirty-five bleeding quid?

RALPH   I have.

JUDD   That had to last me till Wednesday.

ERIC   Feel better after that slash.

JUDD   Thirty-five quid! I didn't even get a kiss or a feel of tit. Pissing hell, I'm depressed.

RALPH   We all are.

ALL   Social comment?

LES   All right, it's up to you . . . I've spent forty quid, next week's board money. My Mam'll have a fit.

ERIC   I've spent . . . er . . . I've forgot what I came out with. I've only got thirty-seven pence left.

JUDD   Yeah, but thirty-five quid.

RALPH   (*hails a taxi*) Taxi! St John's flats . . . waaaaaaay!

LES   Hey look, it's them four birds!

(*Whoops of delight as the taxi arrives. They mime getting into the taxi and it screeches off. They sit moving as though in a car. One of the lads lights a cigarette and begins to smoke. One of the others begins to feel sick.*)

RALPH   I feel sick.

(*The actors convey the sensation that the car is speeding away and taking corners at fast speed. RALPH begins to retch.*)

RALPH   Tell him to stop.

ERIC   I want another slash.

RALPH   Tell him to stop or I'm gonna be sick.

JUDD   (*as though speaking to the driver*) Will you stop? He says he's not stopping 'cos it might be a trick.

ERIC   A trick? What's he want me to do? Rupture my bladder?

LES   I feel a bit spewy. Tell him to slow down.

RALPH   Tell him to stop.

JUDD   I've told him.

LES   Let some air in here. It's like a wrestler's jock strap.

        (ERIC *urinates out of the window. It all blows back into the others' faces.*)

ERIC   I'm doing it out of the window.

LES   Don't be so bloody stupid.

ERIC   Hey lads, I'm slashing out of the window . . .

RALPH   Errm . . . I've been sick down his back.

JUDD   Window . . . dick . . . SHUT! (*He shuts the window.*)

ERIC   Aaaaaargh!

        (*The car suddenly screeches to a halt. Scene switches back to the bouncers at the club.*)

RALPH   Look at the bleeding mess.

ERIC   Animals.

        (JUDD *sings nonsense into the microphone.*)

LES   Look at the amount of beer that's been left. A waste is that, waste.

        (*They stand around contemplating the mess.*)

JUDD	Shall we get packed away and get the video on?
ERIC	Eager tonight Judd, aren't you?
JUDD	I wanna see the filth.
ERIC	You are too sensitive Judd, that's your problem.
RALPH	Look at the mess. Hey there's a pair of knickers over here.
LES	Keep 'em, they might fit you.
JUDD	I'll give you one pound twelve for 'em.
ERIC	Have you seen the bogs?
LES	What's wrong with them?
ERIC	Two urinals cracked, it's all over the floor.
JUDD	What is?
RALPH	(*still rummaging around*) Anybody want a basket meal? One here, still warm.
ERIC	Ah ah . . . look at this.
LES	What?
ERIC	Another fiver.
JUDD	Jammy bastard.
ERIC	That's four nights on the trot.
RALPH	That's why they call him 'lucky' Eric.
JUDD	Are we gerrin' this video on or what?
ERIC	He is a pervert.
RALPH	Well I don't know about you lads, but I'm shagged.
LES	And me.
JUDD	I wish I was.

ERIC   I wish you was and all Judd.

RALPH   I'll tell you this much Eric, I don't think I can stand
           much more of this. It's getting to me. It's all bloody
           getting to me.

ERIC   (*challenges strongly*) That's because you're soft . . .

           (*Silence.*)

RALPH   (*doesn't respond*) Innit peaceful. Listen how quiet it
           is.

JUDD   My ears are still buzzing.

ERIC   My brains buzzing. I think I'm going deaf.

LES   You what?

ERIC   I said I think I'm . . . oh very funny lads. You lads
           are definitely on the ball at this late hour.

JUDD   Are we gerrin this video on or what?

LES   Yeh Ralph get some cans, we'll have a couple of
           hours. Are you stopping Eric?

ERIC   No I'm not a pervert.

JUDD   Ha ha. Look at that. Twenty pence. And it's mine.
           Look he's dying to stop.

ERIC   I wanna get off home.

JUDD   Just watch the first bit.

ERIC   No I . . .

LES   Come on . . .

ERIC   No, I'm not stopping.

JUDD   Come on Eric, spoil yourself.

LES   Yeah, come on.

ERIC   No, I . . .

JUDD   Come on, man . . .

ERIC   Well, ok. I'll stop for the first three hours.

JUDD   Right. Where's that video with animals in it?

LES   Right. Let's get it on.

            (*They put on the imaginary video. It is Michael
            Jackson's "Thriller". Music comes up and the lights
            fade to green, as the bouncers all don monster's
            teeth. They proceed to do a complicated rip-off of
            the Thriller video, moving forwards and backwards,
            grotesquely slouching their shoulders, clapping
            their hands, etc.*)

            [NB: *The Thriller video should be carefully studied
            in order to achieve just the right elements of
            parody. Eventually the lights come up and the music
            stops.*]

JUDD   Who brought that fucking video?

LES   I did.

JUDD   I thought you said it had animals in it.

LES   It did have animals in it.

JUDD   I thought it was shit.

RALPH   Thanks Barry Norman.

            (*The music from the start of the play comes up
            again.*)

ERIC   DOWN AT THE DISCO WAS THE PLACE TO BE
            THE LIGHTS WERE SO BRIGHT
            LIKE A COLOUR TV
            THE MUSIC WAS LOUD
            AND THE BEER FLOWED FREE
            IT WAS A DISCO PLACE FOR YOU AND ME

            ON THE DOOR YOU PAID YOUR MONEY

THE PLACE WAS PACKED
THE PLACE WAS FUNNY
YOU SAW THE GIRLS
MMMMMMM . . . SMELLED THEIR HONEY

THE HEADS WERE HAZY
THE LIMBS WERE LAZY
AND ALL THE YOUNG GIRLS
DANCE LIKE CRAZY
COME ON

BUT NOW ITS OVER YOU GOTTA GO HOME
THERE IS NOWHERE ELSE TO ROAM
BE CAREFUL HOW YOU WALK THE STREETS
THEY'RE THE MEANEST STREETS
IN THE WHOLE DAMN PLACE
IT'S A REAL MEAN STREET
FOR THE HUMAN RACE

AND THROUGH THE BLOOD
AND SNOT AND SEX
MAYBE LOVERS MEET
AND ARE MARRIED NEXT
TWO SPIRITS MOVED
TO HOLD AND CLING
AND THE CHILDREN OF ENGLAND
THEY STILL SING

ALL   HERE WE GO, HERE WE GO, HERE WE GO
HERE WE GO, HERE WE GO, HERE WE GO
HERE WE GO, HERE WE GO, HERE WE GO

WELL FRIDAY NIGHTS AND SATURDAYS TOO
WE'LL BE DOWN HERE, YES WITH YOU AND
YOU
AND THE WHOLE DAMN CREW
IS THERE ANYTHING ELSE TO DO

I said a hip hop
A hippy a hippy
A hip hip hop
AND DON'T YOU STOP!

Blackout.